MARKETING BRAND YOU®

Moving from Chaos to Clarity

LaFern K. Batie, MBA

ACKNOWLEDGEMENTS

This space could hardly capture my gratitude for the love, prayers and encouragement I receive from my family, friends and supporters. I appreciate you more than words can ever express. THANK YOU! In particular, I thank my mother and precious GEM, Ruby; my husband and soul mate, Bob; and my best friend and "mirror holder", Charnessa. I have been richly blessed with an inner circle that lifts me when I am down, pushes me when I need that extra nudge, loves me for who I am and tells me the truth even when it is a bitter pill to swallow. Everyone deserves a "fist" of unwavering supporters like those who pour into my life. I appreciate you! I gratefully acknowledge those who have paved the way for me to even consider this journey. To every reader who is allowing me to share this space with you, THANK YOU!

TABLE OF CONTENTS

PREFACE

"Chaos is merely order waiting to be deciphered."
Jose Saramago (The Double)

Have you ever found yourself wondering how you ended up where you were and being frustrated because you could not clearly see your way out? If so, you can probably relate to what it feels like to be surrounded by, immersed in or confronted by chaos. Perhaps you are in that place right now?

I remember being in that place (and if the truth be told, still occasionally see it rear its ugly head). At one point I was so overwhelmed with everything that I was doing—wife, full-time business leader, full-time graduate student, full-time guardian, household responsibilities, family commitments, civic leadership, professional association memberships, emergency call taker, school shuttle provider... whew! I get tired just thinking about it. You name it and I was allowing myself to be stretched thin by it.

One day, I found myself sitting in a parking lot at the local grocery store. It was a day that I felt like escaping it all and the parking lot was the best that I could do. I was burning the candle at both ends and had another lighter melting the wax in the middle. "How did I end up in the midst of this chaos? How do I get out of this tailspin? Once I am out of it, where in the heck do I go?" These were just a few questions I asked myself while in "parking lot paradise".

I wish I could tell you that I heard a still small voice, saw a bright light, received a revelation or had an "aha" moment. Nope... that did not happen—at least not on that day. However, those "breakaway" moments and the mounting frustration that led to them became more frequent. The grocery store parking lot became my refuge when I could find the time to escape. Often, the only time and space I could find was in my thoughts: "How do I get off of this rollercoaster?"

Eventually, I mustered up the courage to ask myself several critical questions. "If you could escape from this chaotic life, LaFern, where would you go? What would you do? How would you survive? Who would you be?" A new, introspective and uncomfortable phase began in my life. All I really knew was if I wanted a different outcome, I needed a different approach. Where I was at that point in my life was a personal choice resulting from decisions I had made.

Who was I going to be? Hmmm...

What is your earliest and most impactful brand memory? From a branding perspective, if you really think back to the earliest days you can remember, there are people, places, products and experiences that will stay with you forever. What comes to mind for you?

I began my life surrounded by family, strong community, fun and the sun of Ocean City, Maryland—west Ocean City to be exact. Having lived there for my first five years and visiting for many more to follow, one fond memory that stands out among so many others is my paternal grandmother's cooking. Whether I was shimmying my way onto the red vinyl covered stool at her restaurant's counter or comfortably perched on a chair at the metal-trimmed table in her small, immaculate kitchen, her delectable delights danced on my taste buds, filled my heart with love and nourished my spirit. Of course, I thought the special touch that she added was just for me. Little did I know, but my grandmother spread her legacy of love throughout the community.

A few years ago, I bumped into a lady who also grew up in our community. I often played with her children and spent many days in her mother's home. As we reminisced about our individual memories, she fondly and specifically recalled the delicious meals that my grandmother prepared over the years. We laughed about the well-seasoned, golden fried chicken, sautéed cabbage and perfectly cooked long grain white rice. You see, her memories were rooted in a different, yet equally impactful, experience. In addition to her visits to the restaurant, she especially remembered the meals that my grandmother quietly and lovingly delivered to her parents and all of the children during tough economic times.

What makes this lady's story so memorable is that it was over 30 years after my grandmother's death. Consistently, when I connect with family, friends and neighbors who have experienced my grandmother's love on a plate, they recount similar stories and memories. Not only did my grandmother's meals seep into the remembrance of countless others, but her legacy lives on for years afterward.

Often, our most powerful life lessons come from experiences that are near and dear to us. The more I learn and grow, the more I appreciate the rich insights and guidance provided even when I was not aware of the significance they would have on who I am. My grandparents, parents, aunts, uncles, extended family and neighbors are blocks on this quilt that has become my life experience. With names unrecognized by the world, but precious to so many who knew and still know them, I celebrate the village that helped shape that brand called "ME"!

I dedicate this book, *Marketing Brand You®: Moving from Chaos to Clarity*, to my petite, powerhouse, paternal grandmother, Estelle Kitt Tyler, one of the strongest, longest living personal brands I know!

LaFern

CHAPTER 1

· · · · · · · · · · · · · · · · · ·

INTRODUCTION TO BRANDING

"What you do speaks so loud that I cannot hear what you say."
Ralph Waldo Emerson

If I asked you to quickly share five words to describe who you are, could you do it? How about if I asked you to share the value that you bring to those who encounter you—how comfortable would you be providing those descriptors?

On a scale from one to ten, with ten being completely comfortable and confident, how would you rate yourself when it comes down to talking about you, your value, contributions and accomplishments? If you have rated yourself less than a ten—or, for that matter, nowhere near it—this is the resource for you. *Marketing Brand You®—Moving from Chaos to Clarity*—is a practical, step-by-step approach to help you fully understand your brand, the value that you provide and how to strengthen it in order to help others recognize, experience and appreciate that value.

Before we begin this branding exploration, let me be very clear about what I mean by "branding". Branding is not simply about the image that you project. It is the substance that you possess, experiences that others have with you and the legacy that you create in everything that you do. Here's the kicker: if your brand is inconsistent in one area of your life, it is being compromised. One key to branding is consistency! Wherever you show up, whatever you communicate, however you behave, whatever you speak—it is all a part of the brand called YOU!

Be it as a business owner, organizational leader, professional, student, volunteer, family member or general citizen, you and those around you represent the brands that are reflected in corporations and other organizations of all types. Organizations represent the individuals within them. The larger brand's power is experienced one person, product or service at a time. It is no wonder that branding remains a buzz word in our business and social lexicons. The ripple effect is tremendous!

Many years ago, I was an eager accounting undergraduate student who lived by the syllabus and stacks of textbooks. They were my lifelines to higher learning—or at least that is what I thought. You know the drill, right? At least this is how it used to work back in the "old" days. You registered for class (by showing up on campus and standing in long lines) and received your textbook and resource list. On the first day of class, you showed up, met your professor and fellow classmates, nestled into a comfortable spot and waited on the document that you lived by—the golden SYLLABUS!

Well, here it was... day one of my marketing class. As I patiently listened to the normal introductory lecture, I wondered why there were no textbooks for the class—no articles list, case studies and the normal muscle building materials that I had grown accustomed to. The professor began by sharing the unique project we each would be responsible for researching and understanding throughout the semester. With a slight smile, he said, "This is a product you will be quite familiar with. However, you are not nearly as familiar with it as you will be by the end of this class." Huh? How could he be so sure *everyone* in the class would be familiar with this product? With students ranging from 19 to 50, surely we *all* could not possibly be familiar with this one market item.

"Your primary research project for this semester will be you." We looked suspiciously at one another with furrowed brows and questioning eyes. "Yes, you," he reiterated. "You will be embarking upon one of the greatest journeys of your life as you prepare to leave this university. Your primary mission will be to position yourselves for the absolute best professional opportunities you can create. But how will you do that if you do not thoroughly and completely understand who you are and why an organization will want you to help contribute to its success."

Wow... no textbooks! Was he serious? I would spend the entire semester researching, studying, preparing and positioning myself? I was just a little disappointed—really, I was. What then seemed like such an unconventional burden was one of the greatest blessings of my educational and professional experience.

Often, I meet leaders and professionals who desire more in their careers and businesses than they are currently experiencing. The very opportunities they were once excited about leave them wanting, searching and desiring an often ill-defined "more". The dream job might feel like a nightmare some days. You might be one who was once so energized by your new business. Economic dips, tight budgets, cost conscious customers and rapidly changing markets have sucked the life out of your once full sail. As one client so emphatically stated, "I do not know what I want but I am sure it's not this."

It makes no difference where you are right now. What matters is that you are obviously committed to taking the action required to strengthen your brand—to intentionally impact the experience that others have with you. Welcome... it is my pleasure to walk on this journey with you.

LaFern

CHAPTER 2

· · · · · · · · · · · · · · · · · ·

WHAT'S IN A BRAND?

"A personal brand is an identity that stimulates precise, meaningful perceptions in its audience about the values and qualities that a person stands for."
Peter Montoya

What do you think of when you hear the following?

- "Mmm mmm good"
- "Just do it"
- "Good to the last drop"
- "Quality is job one"

Campbell's soup? Nike? Maxwell House coffee? Ford? You are correct! What is it about those slogans that imprint them into our memories? The first step to recognizing a brand is familiarity—intentional familiarity, also known as marketing. We did not just stumble across those names. They were intentionally introduced and continually communicated to us in a way that makes them memorable and familiar. That is what you need your brand to be in order to effectively compete for opportunities in this increasingly challenging and globally competitive environment—value that is consistent and familiar.

Let's go on a trip to the store to pick up a few items needed at home. Before you even get to the store, you probably have an idea of which store you prefer. What are a few factors that will influence your decision?

- *Location*—proximity to your home, convenient access, parking, store design, near other places that you need to go;
- *Offerings*—product variety, pricing, current sales, in-stock items;
- *Service*—friendly and helpful staff, quick check-out, easy to find items, assistance with loading items into your vehicle;
- *Preference*—it is simply where you have always shopped (besides, your mother shopped there for years!).

Think about it... before you purchase one item these are just a few considerations that you consciously or subconsciously make.

Now, you have arrived at the store. Walk down any given aisle and you will see dozens of different brands for the same product type. So, what makes you choose one soft drink over another? One soap for your baby versus another? One brand or type of soup when you have a cold? Every day, we repeatedly make selections based on our preferences and experiences. How does this apply to your brand? Similarly, every day, we choose whether or not to engage with others, select them for an assignment, purchase their product or service, refer them to a prospective client, recommend them to an employer, recognize their efforts, share information, ask for assistance or solicit feedback. Guess what? They make the same considerations when it comes to you.

A brand is an *identity* designed to differentiate—to set apart.

What makes you or your business different? Without differentiation, we have homogeneity—no way to distinguish one person, product or service from another. How much time are you investing in understanding who you are, how you uniquely do what you do and what differentiates you from someone else versus blending into the crowd?

A brand is an *emotional* promise of an *experience*.

Every factor—name, reputation, logo, visual appeal and experience with the commodity (person, product or service)—contributes to the emotional connection that you have with a brand. This experience reflects how you deliver what you promise—or not.

Nearly fifteen years ago, I was shopping in one of my favorite department stores for perfume during the Christmas holiday season. As you might imagine, customers were everywhere. One apparently overwhelmed salesperson was responsible for serving the rapidly expanding crowd that encircled the counter. After waiting for quite some time, I decided to go to the opposite end of the mall to a different store that I had heard about but never frequented. Well, what an experience! Sales assistants were plentiful, but not overbearing. The store was very well organized. A tuxedoed gentleman played the piano softly and they had the perfume that I wanted. As I eyed the shoes just across the aisle, the sales assistant said, "Miss, if you'd like, you may have a seat and we will have someone assist you with finding the perfect pair of shoes, while we wrap the perfume and bring it to you." I sat in a comfy chair, described my shoe, was brought several options, sipped hot cider, and paid for my items—all without moving another inch! On that day, I became a loyal customer.

A brand is built on a set of *core values* or features.

Whatever is most important to you shows up in your brand. It is what you become known for, intentionally or unintentionally. For example, if you are always late, rushing to get to most places on time, then that might be part of your brand. Sometimes, we assign a comfortable classification to our tardiness such as "fashionably late". What does it really say about us and what we value? How do others feel when they are waiting for us? Do they simply plan accordingly because that is what they have been conditioned to expect? As a recovering rusher who wanted to squeeze all that I could out of every minute of the day, I share that example first hand. What motivated me to change? Knowing that those who were waiting could justifiably consider my tardiness as a rude and disrespectful gesture. Changing one's perceived brand is a conscious decision requiring specific action.

Let's have some fun! Spend the next 30 seconds identifying as many of these brands as you can.

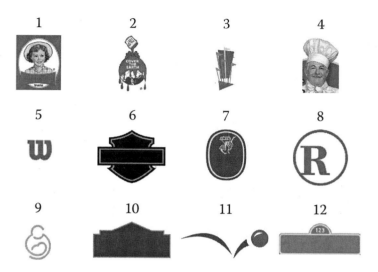

Were you able to identify all of them? Let's see...

1. Little Debbie®
2. Sherwin-Williams®
3. Six Flags®
4. Chef Boyardee®
5. Wilson®
6. Harley-Davidson®
7. Chiquita®
8. Radio Shack®
9. March of Dimes®
10. Lowe's®
11. PetSmart®
12. Sesame Street®

What is the point of this exercise? We can easily identify many logos, mascots and their respective names in the general market-place—even if that logo or mascot is not the most current one in use. Of course, you have a much more intimate connection with yourself, so shouldn't you be significantly well-versed in Brand YOU? More than anyone else, everything about who you are or what your business represents should be reflected in how you show up and what you deliver.

EXCAVATION EXERCISE

What is one of your favorite brands?

_____

_____

_____

_____

What influences your brand loyalty?

_____

_____

_____

_____

CHAPTER 3

· · · · · · · · · · · · · · · · · · ·

UNVEILING BRAND YOU

"Act as if what you do makes a difference. It does."
William James

Before we delve into your brand strength, let's talk about a key factor that is the foundation for Marketing Brand YOU®... CONFIDENCE. Often, I work with clients in understanding how their confidence, or lack thereof, shapes their ability to attract success. Diminished confidence sometimes shows up in the following ways: dismissing compliments, disliking tasks (e.g. sales, finance and networking) and remaining in less-than-desirable, yet comfortable, personal and professional situations. There is no quick fix to building or re-building self-confidence; however, it can be achieved through a deliberate process that begins with preparing for the journey.

On the scale below, identify how comfortable you are communicating about who you are and the value you provide by placing an "X" on the line:

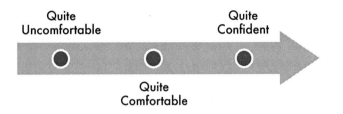

Quite
Uncomfortable

Quite
Confident

Quite
Comfortable

If you are less than "Quite Confident", what are the factors that contribute to lacking or diminished confidence or discomfort when it comes to sharing your value with others?

☐ I feel as if I am bragging about myself.

☐ I am not clear about the value that I provide to others.

☐ It is up to others to talk about my accomplishments and value.

☐ I really do not see how I provide value that is different from someone else who does what I do.

☐ I want to do something new and different and I have no track record in that area.

☐ I have never thought of myself as a brand.

What other reasons are you less than fully confident?

Here are a few helpful tips to remember when it comes to talking about your brand:

1. **It is not *just* about you.** It is about the value that others receive from what you do or provide. When you are pursuing a client, interviewing for a position, being considered for a promotion or trying to develop new relationships, no matter how wonderful your personality or charming your style (although both can be quite beneficial), what your prospective client, employer or connection really wants to know is the mutual or sole benefit that you will provide.

2. **Talk about your value in terms of how others have benefitted.** This can be based on feedback that you have received or solicited. What have others told you about the value you delivered to them?

3. **Really listen to the compliments given to you by others.** These can be clear indicators that others perceive value that you create in those areas. The following examples will further clarify what to listen for:

    a. Others talk about how skilled you are in a particular area (e.g. "You are so gifted at concisely and clearly communicating the challenges.");

    b. You are routinely sought for your expertise (e.g. "We need someone with your sales expertise and relationship-building skills to train our new associates.");

c. A product or resource that you have created is in demand, widely used or regularly requested (e.g. "Can you provide to the team copies of the planning template that you created?"); or

d. You are asked to work on certain problems because of your expertise (e.g. "We can always rely on you to help get our problem programs back on track").

4. **Be prepared.** It is great when others openly and willingly share their positive experiences they have had with your brand. It is prudent to be prepared to share when someone asks you a question as simple as, "So tell me... what do you do?" We typically provide a list of tasks that we engage in rather than how what we do provides value for someone else. If someone is really interested in learning more about how we can help them, wouldn't it be great to help them "see" that value? Consider this simplified example:

Automobile X	
General	Specific
Good gas mileage	Economical—43 miles per gallon
Good price	Great value $5,000 less than comparable vehicles; high resale value—55% of original price
Perfect size	Comfortably seats five adults ; Rear legroom—40.2"; front legroom—42.6"

5. No one is a mirror image of you. Even with two people who have similar skills, knowledge and experiences, there are differences in the way that they do what they do.

Sharing your value with those who have an interest in you, your products or your services does not have to sound like a scripted sales pitch or a brag list. A simple way to communicate your value can be as basic as restating what others have shared with you:

"Clients that I have worked with often tell me that I help them simplify seemingly large challenges by breaking them into small, manageable parts. In doing so, they meet or exceed their performance goals by staying focused without being overwhelmed. Some clients have told me that they have reduced the amount of time spent on their projects by as much as 40%."

Does that sound like bragging or is more of a testimonial based on what you have delivered and how your clients have benefitted as a result? You have simply re-communicated a value-based testimonial!

EXCAVATION EXERCISE

What do others tell you that you do well?

_____

_____

_____

_____

_____

_____

_____

_____

_____

When do others typically compliment you?

_____

_____

_____

_____

_____

_____

_____

_____

_____

CHAPTER 4

· · · · · · · · · · · · · · · · · · ·

YOUR BRAND STRENGTH

"In the last analysis, what we are communicates far more eloquently than anything we say or do."
Stephen Covey

The best way to determine what you need to do to maximize your brand is to first identify your current brand strength. This is a quick assessment that will give you a general idea about your current personal or organizational state.

Brand Strength	YES	NO
Have you clearly documented your personal mission, the results when executed and who it will impact?		
Can you state your five most relevant and compelling attributes—adjectives that describe you?		
Have you identified and documented short- and long-term goals that motivate you to take action?		
Can you state your top five values—the non-negotiable values that influence your decisions?		
Do you review your goals and track your progress no less than quarterly?		
Do you know what others would say is your greatest strength?		
When others introduce you, do they use the same words that you would use to describe yourself?		
Are you clear about your most significant personal obstacles—those limitations that could hold you back from achieving your goals?		
Do you know how your self-perception differs from the perceptions that others have of you?		
Do you understand the value that you offer and what distinguishes you from others with similar skills, knowledge and experiences?		
Can you clearly describe your target audience—those who value what you offer?		
Do you have at least one mentor, professional coach, sponsor and/or professional advisory board?		
Does your visual, verbal and nonverbal presentation have a favorable effect on others?		
Do you mark every project with your personal brand (e.g. meetings, reports, team projects, presentations)?		

Brand Strength	YES	NO
Do you have strong internal and external professional networks?		
Do you communicate regularly with members of your network (e.g. e-mail, telephone conversations, in person)?		
Does your personal appearance or style reflect what you want others to see and is it appropriate for your target audience?		
Does your work environment reflect your desired brand?		
Do you serve in a leadership role if you are a member of a professional organization?		
Do you routinely seek feedback from peers, managers or clients to help improve your performance?		

Count the total number of "YES" responses.

'Yes' Responses	

17-20	You have a strong, leading brand. *Congratulations!*
14-16	You are making good progress. *Keep moving forward!*
0-13	You have what it takes to build a solid brand. *Let's implement a plan!*

Do not get hung up on the score! This is a self-assessment—not a test that determines whether or not you have passed or failed in life. On our paths to success, it is critical that we occasionally check to see how we are progressing. Consider this your **BGPS**—

Brand Global Positioning System! Sometimes, I use a GPS even when I am in a familiar environment but I am unsure about how to get to the specific address. I kind of, sort of know where I am but to ensure that I do not get completely off track, waste time, become frustrated and possibly become unnecessarily stressed, I follow the clear directions communicated to me. When I make a wrong turn or encounter a detour, my GPS recalculates the route and I follow it.

Here is something to ponder... a brand simply IS. Whether or not you invest time and attention in developing and shaping your brand, it still exists. Others have perceptions, experiences and opinions relating to you and your organization. Ignoring your brand does not change its impact. The key to your continued success is to recognize your brand's potential and how you can leverage it to help you soar higher!

Are you ready? Let's get started!

CHAPTER 5

. . . .

SOLID GROUND OR SINK HOLE?

"There are no secrets to success. It is the result of preparation, hard work, and learning from failure."
Gen. Colin Powell, USA (Ret.)

Would you ever knowingly build a home that sat on land just above a sink hole—where the surface beneath has dissolved, is hollow and can no longer support the structure? Regardless of how wonderful the property appeared to be, if you knew that the land beneath could swallow the home at any time, I doubt that you would purchase it.

According to the U.S. Geological Survey, sinkholes generally form over time and are caused by rock, like limestone, being dissolved by naturally flowing water. Over time, this causes underground caves and cavities. When the caves and cavities collapse, sinkholes form, jeopardizing whatever sits on the surface. Additionally, humans can speed up this natural process by rapidly pumping groundwater and drinking water from beneath the surface, causing the caves and cavities to form at an increased rate. Now, what does this have to do with your business or professional brand? Through natural shifts such as changing demand for our knowledge, skills, services or products, technological advances, restructured organizations, obsolete products, increased competition and decreased resources, it is realistic to expect that the foundation on which your career or business was built needs to be reevaluated and strengthened in order for you to remain competitive and be positioned for long-term success.

Similar to the need for a strong, solid foundation when constructing a physical structure, you must exercise the same care when building your business or career. Thoroughly understanding and being able to articulate who you are and what you offer that others might value is a core component of your personal foundation. How much time have you spent—let's say within the past year—really understanding what distinguishes you from everyone else? What motivates you to do what you do, giving you a sense of purpose?

Think about the word 'vocation.' When you hear it, what do you immediately think of? According to Merriam-Webster, 'vocation' shares the Latin root 'vocare' with words such as voice, vocal and evoke. It is defined as a calling or a strong inner impulse toward a particular course of action. When you think about that definition and your present career or business, do you feel a strong sense of purpose and calling or are you frustrated, overwhelmed and wondering how you arrived at this point? The clearer your thoughts are about what pulls you forward, personally and professionally, the more likely you are to spend your time in roles and ventures that fulfill—not drain—you. That is where your true passion and talents will shine through. As we grow as leaders and individuals, why not maximize our talents in situations that simultaneously and optimally benefit us, our clients and the organizations we serve?

EXCAVATION EXERCISE

What do you think you do better than most people?

_____

_____

_____

_____

_____

_____

How is your environment (i.e. people, relationships, productivity) different because of your contributions?

_____

_____

_____

_____

_____

_____

CHAPTER 6

. . . .

WHAT HAVE YOU DONE LATELY?

"If what you are doing is not moving you towards your goals, then it's moving you away from your goals."
Brian Tracy

If asked, "Who are you", how do you respond? Do you respond with your job title and responsibilities? Or do you describe yourself in relationship to others (e.g. parent, sibling, employee, XYZ business owner)?

Who are you? Your true identity is established from the inside out, beginning with your core being (the real you), values, attributes, motivations, aspirations, accomplishments and image. Yes, image. Regardless of whether or not your efforts are intentional or unintentional, how you project yourself becomes others' definition of who you are. While I did not begin with image, it is important and shapes perceptions.

Who do you aspire to be?

Have you ever asked children what they want to be when they grow up? Often, they will respond quickly and confidently with answers reflecting what they enjoy doing most. You might get a response encompassing all current interests—a doctor, ballerina and a teacher! There is little that can dissuade them when their minds are focused on what they love—or at least what they think they love based on their self-perception about their ability to *be* that role. Not only do they tell you but they immerse themselves in *being*. For instance, if little Jasmine says she wants to be a doctor, she immediately begins acting like one. She has a stethoscope around her neck (or something that functions as one), checking on any person or stuffed animal who is willing to be the patient. She might even have a little bag with "pretend" (a.k.a. candy) medications. It seems that with time and external influences their desires shift from what they enjoy most.

What do we have to learn from these young, open minds?

- **Give attention to who you desire to be.** Know what you want to accomplish. You do not have to wait until you get into the role to begin honing the skills that you will need. What are your goals for the next 90 days? Six months? Year? *Write them down* and *be specific* about what you want to achieve.

- **Shape your reality with your thoughts, words and behaviors.** Invest time thinking about your desires, write your vision and take action to grow both your knowledge and your expertise. Be honest about your skills and developmental needs.

- **Take action!** One little step at a time is often what is needed most. Do not become trapped by inaction. Action does not have to be a huge, overwhelming leap. It can be as simple as reading an article or book to get focused and learn more about your interest area.

A successful brand is built on known skills, talents and accomplishments. It is easy to overlook your past progress and accomplishments if you do not consciously conduct a personal inventory. Sometimes, our current challenges distract us, causing us to lose focus of experiences that have helped us progress to this stage. Let's intentionally look at the valuable gems in your experience treasure chest.

List your five most significant professional skills and accomplishments:

1. _____

_____

_____

2. _____

_____

_____

3. _____

_____

_____

4. _____

_____

_____

5. _____

_____

_____

Do you need a memory jogger to capture those accomplishments and skills? This list might be a good jump start.

Skills & Accomplishments	
Awards received	Challenges resolved
Creative solutions	Public speaking
Crisis management	Records set
Diplomatic success	Strong references
Financial success	Language proficiency
Leadership roles	Unique talents
Interpersonal success	Reputation among peers

How can you use what you already know to reach your current goals?

_____

_____

_____

_____

_____

_____

_____

_____

_____

_____

_____

_____

You have proven that you have significant value and considerable substance. Keep this list with you. When you are feeling frustrated or disappointed, review it as a reminder of your capabilities.

⛏ EXCAVATION EXERCISE

What single action are you willing to take to move closer to your aspirations?

_____
_____
_____
_____
_____
_____
_____
_____
_____

List five people who can support you on your journey:

1. _____

2. _____

3. _____

4. _____

5. _____

· · · · · · · · · · · · · · · · · · ·

CHAPTER 7

VALUE BEYOND MEASURE

*"Personal leadership is the process of keeping your
vision and values before you and aligning your life to be
congruent with them."*
Stephen Covey

What do you value? Values are ideals that are personally important and meaningful to you. They are your guiding principles and are central to your beliefs. We all have them. They are specific and individual yet we often share similar values with others, particularly those in our innermost circles. Goals that align with our values often bring fulfillment. Your values:

- Reflect your personal philosophy;
- Resonate deeply with you;
- Are considered "core" values if we cannot imagine functioning without them.

What motivates you?

What really drives you to do what you do day in and day out?

Whether or not you have consciously evaluated who you really are, what you value most, your motivators, or who you aspire to be, you can often tell whether or not they all align with how you are currently investing your life based on what you think about your current circumstances.

The following list contains common core values. Review the list and circle the core values that resonate most with you. If there are descriptors that are not included, add them. After you have identified that list, select the **top FIVE.**

Core Values		
Abundance	Family	Perfection
Accomplishment	Flexibility	Persistence
Accountability	Freedom	Personal growth
Accuracy	Friendship	Power
Advancement	Fulfillment	Practicality
Adventure	Fun	Professionalism
Authenticity	Giving	Progress
Balance	Gratitude	Punctuality
Beauty	Growth	Rationality
Catalyze	Harmony	Recognition
Challenge	Honesty	Reliability

Core Values		
Collaboration	Honor	Relationship
Coaching	Humility	Resilience
Commitment	Inclusion	Respect
Community	Independence	Responsibility
Compassion	Ingenuity	Safety
Competence	Innovation	Satisfying others
Competition	Inspiration	Security
Control	Integrity	Service
Creativity	Joy	Sincerity
Decisiveness	Justice	Skillfulness
Determination	Kindness	Status
Discipline	Knowledge	Strength
Discovery	Leadership	Structure
Diversity	Learning	Success
Education	Love	Teaching
Effectiveness	Loyalty	Tolerance
Efficiency	Money	Tradition
Empathy	Openness	Trust
Equality	Optimism	Truth
Excellence	Originality	Wealth
Faith	Passion	Wellness
Fame	Peace	Wisdom

For each core value (top five), describe how it is currently reflected in what you do.

Core Value #1:

Description:

_____

_____

_____

_____

_____

Core Value #2:

Description:

_____

_____

_____

_____

Core Value #3:

Description:

_____

_____

_____

_____

_____

Core Value #4:

Description:

_____

_____

_____

_____

_____

Core Value #5:

Description:

_____

_____

_____

_____

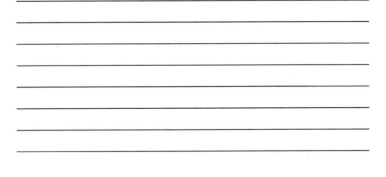

EXCAVATION EXERCISE

Identify one gap between your core values and your current practices. For example, if 'wellness' is a core value, yet you are not making time for regular exercise daily, that is a gap.

_____

_____

_____

_____

_____

_____

_____

What one action could you take to narrow the gap? It could be something as simple as walking for ten minutes each day during your lunch break or parking farther away at the grocery store in order to get in more steps.

_____

_____

_____

_____

_____

_____

_____

CHAPTER 8

MIRROR, MIRROR ON THE WALL

"When your image improves, your performance improves."
Zig Ziglar

How do you think others describe you when you are not in the room?

Do they use the same words that you use?

You are a total package. In addition to your intrinsic values, motivators, self-perceptions and beliefs, your package includes the following:

- Appearance;
- Verbal communication;
- Non-verbal communication;
- General behaviors.

You create a total experience for others. It begins with what they see when they look at you—the obvious, what you present. However, your package is not limited to your appearance. It includes layers just beyond the obvious such as how and what you communicate. For example, when you are approached by someone new in a networking setting, how do you respond? Do you engage? Retreat? Dominate the conversation? Ask questions and listen to learn more about that person? Do you extend a limp hand or a confident, firm grasp?

How do you show up? Your appearance speaks volumes about your attention to detail and the current state of your life. By the way, this extends beyond your physical appearance to areas including your work area and automobile. The next time you are preparing to be in others' presence—going to work, a meeting, a conference—take one minute for a "once over" evaluation. Stand in the mirror and honestly assess what you see. Do you project what you want others to perceive?

A client recently shared her experience at a professional association conference. While there, she attended a reception comprised of numerous prospective service providers for her organization. Immediately, she connected with the most polished and professional looking attendees. Does that mean that the others would not deliver excellent services or products? No, but in reality our first impression often shapes our perception of who others are and what they can deliver.

Do you have a mirror nearby? Seriously... if you do, I want you to get up, take this book with you, and walk to the mirror. If it is a full-length mirror, that is even better. What do you see when you look at your reflection? Do you see in yourself what you want others to see in you? This is not about whether you are impeccably dressed and polished right now. While we want others to see us at our best, what they see goes far beyond the superficial.

Merriam-Webster defines an image as a "visual representation of something". What does your "visual representation" reflect? Your image—your package—outwardly reflects your brand. As I previously mentioned, it includes your visual appearance, nonverbal communication, verbal communication and behaviors.

Your image:

- Creates a lasting first impression;
- Helps define the message that you send to others;
- Communicates about you, your products and your services;
- Establishes a relationship that is not necessarily about your position in an organization.

I have been richly blessed with great advice that I have earnestly listened to throughout my life. Sometimes, it took several attempts for me to really get the message. However, the following wise words only had to penetrate my brain once—and I have never forgotten them:

"Show up for the role you want, not the one you have."

Imagine searching for a home. You might be a person who can see a house with neglected landscaping, peeling paint, stained flooring, aging appliances and a dated decor and recognize tremendous potential. You immediately visualize the possibilities—flowers, trees, shrubs, partial brick façade, vibrant wall colors, hardwood floors, marble flooring, granite countertops and stainless steel appliances. What an exciting project this will be!!

If the mere thought leaves you exhausted, perhaps you are more comfortable walking into a home that appears to require only you and your personal items. You are greeted at the door by a freshly baked apple pie fragrance. The living spaces are immaculate, meticulously arranged and tastefully decorated. Natural sunlight warmly fills the open spaces. You immediately feel at home.

Does that same process apply to the way we see others—and how they see us? Of course it does! We are not guaranteed that someone will take the time to look past our exteriors to see the potential we have. Your first impression is the most important one. With so many competitors seeking opportunities and clients, can you really afford not to give extra effort to making your first encounter—be it live or virtual—a positive one?

Fair or unfair, packaging is important. Now, when I refer to image and packaging, I am not talking about how much you invest in clothing or whose name is on the label. I am talking about how you present yourself in order to impact others' perceptions in order to access opportunities that you desire. Companies spend billions of dollars on logos, redesigned packaging and tweaked slogans—all in the name of generating a positive emotional experience for its current and prospective customers (i.e. branding).

Everyone has a preferred style which is captured in his or her visual presentation. While numerous experts offer image consulting services, it is not a necessary investment to refine your projected image. Many department and specialty stores offer complimentary services to help you select your best look for your needs and budget. One visit might be all that you need. If you desire to work with a professional image consultant, research their success with past customers and ask for referrals from others who have used similar services. Solicit feedback on personal shoppers or utilize free sessions and workshops often offered to introduce prospective clients to their services.

Extensive research has shown that you have seven seconds— yes, *seven*—to make a first impression! While you might not consciously think about it, you instinctively and immediately assess what is before you. Historically, that is how we subconsciously function as humans. It is similar to whether or not your adrenaline rushes, sending you into fight or flight mode, when you feel safe or threatened.

Professor Albert Mehrabian, a pioneer in the communications field, shared his findings about the importance of words and non-verbal cues over 40 years ago in his book *Silent Messages*. Mehrabian's study, simplified, unveiled how people respond to facial expressions, the way words are spoken and the actual words that are used. This study applied to communications involving feelings and attitudes. Remember, branding is an *emotional* promise of an experience. (If you doubt that, try to make a loyal Coke fan drink Pepsi or vice versa and see how much emotion is involved!)

People respond based on these criteria:

- 55% What they see/facial expression
- 38% How you speak/how words are spoken
- 7% What you say/words spoken

It is important that your verbal and nonverbal communications align, especially when dealing with emotions.

What does your image communicate?

- Trustworthy
- Reliable
- Energetic
- Innovative
- Confident
- Uncertain
- Empathetic
- Indifferent

Sometimes we need to realign our self-perceptions. Many years ago, I was talking with a trusted advisor about how I perceived myself. "I walk into the room, blend in and tend to be low-keyed when connecting with others." Well, was I in for a surprise!

"Is that what you think people see?" my advisor asked.

"Of course," I replied with a questioning look.

In his typical matter-of-fact style, he responded, "Let me tell you what I see, LaFern. You enter the room with a healthy dose of confidence. In a no-nonsense way, you speak, exchange minimal pleasantries and jump right into the work at hand. We know you mean business when you arrive. That is good but if your goal is to develop relationships, then you need to give more attention to doing just that."

Wow! What surprising feedback that was. I did not expect it but was grateful to have received it—even if it was a bitter pill to swallow.

Was this the impression that I wanted to make? Absolutely not! While I value hard work, focused efforts and high productivity, my image did not reflect how much I valued the relationships. I consciously changed my approach—not to be someone who I am not but to align my behaviors and style with what is truly most important to me.

I greatly appreciate the insights provided to me that allow me to increase my effectiveness and operate in full integrity.

EXCAVATION EXERCISE

What image or package do you currently present to others?

_____

_____

_____

_____

_____

What changes, if any, do you desire to make to realign those perceptions?

_____

_____

_____

_____

_____

Who is a trusted advisor you can ask to help you see yourself as others see you?

_____

_____

_____

_____

_____

CHAPTER 9

· · · · · · · · · · · · · · · · · ·

PERCEPTION'S POWER

"The optimist sees the donut, the pessimist sees the hole."
Oscar Wilde

Let's get real. While your brand is comprised of your core values, personal attributes, motivations, skills and experiences, most people who encounter you will make an immediate judgment based on what they see and how you behave.

Think of one person whom you really admire. What is it about that individual that evokes such feelings? Early in my career, I had the honor and pleasure of working on a team led by one of the most effective leaders that I have known. While I was, and remain, impressed with his professional experiences and achievements, how he lived his core values helped shape the leader that I became. He treated everyone on the team with respect, showing genuine interest in each person's progress regardless of position. With the discipline that one might expect from a retired military leader, he led a balanced life, making time nearly every day for lunch with his wife. While learning about leadership effectiveness through my reading and studies has been helpful, seeing it in practice impacted me immeasurably. If I had to define it in one sentence, his leadership, discipline, family-orientation, community service and respect for others are key attributes reflected in his brand.

How do others describe you, particularly when you are not in their presence?

Just as commodities exchanged on the free market are identified by their attributes, image and packaging, so are we.

Which brands do you associate with the following descriptors?

- Safe, luxury automobile
- No frills, go anywhere, value airline
- Delivers on time packages
- Prepares accurate tax returns
- Sells gourmet coffee

I sometimes use this exercise when facilitating workshops. Without exception, the responses differ for every descriptor. Why? It is all a matter of perception and each participant's experiences. There are no right or wrong answers. It is all about PERCEPTION.

Brand attributes describe your promise of value—what others can expect you to deliver. Review the following list. Circle the attributes that resonate most with you. If other attributes describe

you more accurately, please add them to the list below. Select your
top **FIVE** attributes.

Personal Brand Attributes		
Accessible	Entrepreneurial	Perceptive
Accurate	Ethical	Pessimistic
Action-oriented	Extroverted	Philanthropic
Aggressive	Fair	Political
Aloof	Firm	Practical
Arrogant	Flexible	Proactive
Ambitious	Forceful	Procrastinating
Analytical	Friendly	Productive
Apathetic	Generous	Professional
Assertive	Genuine	Realistic
Attractive	Healthy	Rebellious
Bold	Honest	Receptive
Brash	Humorous	Reliable
Charismatic	Imaginative	Responsible
Collaborative	Indecisive	Resourceful
Competitive	Innovative	Ruthless
Confident	Insensitive	Sincere
Conscientious	Insightful	Sophisticated
Consistent	Inspiring	Shy
Conservative	Intelligent	Spiritual
Controlling	Intense	Strategic
Creative	Introverted	Supportive
Decisive	Intuitive	Tactical

Personal Brand Attributes		
Dependable	Knowledgeable	Tenacious
Detailed	Logical	Thoughtful
Diplomatic	Loyal	Tolerant
Direct	Materialistic	Trusting
Driven	Mature	Trustworthy
Efficient	Optimistic	Understanding
Eloquent	Organized	Versatile
Empathetic	Passionate	Visionary
Energetic	Persuasive	Wise

A successful brand is focused and should reflect what you want others to immediately associate with you. They could also be referred to as your "product features". Having a clear focus on external perceptions will help you strengthen your brand.

How confident are you in your assessment of how others perceive you? Don't have any idea? Try this exercise to help guide your development:

- Ask five colleagues and/or trusted advisors to identify your personal brand attributes by providing five words that describe how they see you;

- Do not include those who hesitate to be objective or feel obligated to tell you what they think you want to hear;

- Compare the responses to your list.

How similar were their responses to yours?

What attributes did your colleagues and trusted advisors provide that surprised you?

🧗 EXCAVATION EXERCISE

Which external perceptions do you desire to reshape?

_____

_____

_____

_____

_____

What are you specifically willing to do to reshape those perceptions?

_____

_____

_____

_____

_____

In 90 days, reassess the external perceptions to determine how much progress you have made. This will give you an opportunity to evaluate the feedback and tweak your brand accordingly.

CHAPTER 10

• • • • • • • • • • • • • • • • • •

WHO IS IN YOUR INNERMOST CIRCLE?

"Lots of people want to ride with you in the limo, but what you want is someone who will take the bus with you when the limo breaks down."
Oprah Winfrey

Success is not a solitary pursuit. On your leadership journey, you will need others to support, guide and collaborate with you. (By the way, I use leadership to describe HOW you do what you do and not simply the position you occupy.) Look around you. *Who is on your team?*

Think about what you aspire to do and who you desire to be. Who, in your innermost circle, has already "been there, done that" or has the skills to help you get there? That is not to say they have been *exactly* where you are going but they have achieved success on a level that you want to experience it or can be a powerful accountability partner.

Personal Advisory Board

Are you the top achiever in your circle? If so, you already know what I am going to say… it is time to expand your team or get a new one. This team will have skills, competencies, experiences and exposure that will complement yours. A Personal Advisory Board consists of individuals who care as much about you as they do your pursuits. They will tell you the truth even when you do not want to hear it. You can trust them.

As with anyone you ask to support you personally or professionally, it is important that you share and agree on expectations.

- What are you trying to accomplish?
- In what specific ways can they support you?
- How often would you like to engage?
- *What can you do to support them or something they are passionate about?*

Does this team convene formally? Not necessarily. These resources may support you individually or collectively. It does not matter what you call them, how many you have or whether it is a formal group. What matters is that you engage others at various levels to create an effective team, including mentors and coaches. However, be willing to support and give back to them. Partnerships are reciprocal by definition—and this is a practical way to form powerful partnerships. Remember, this is not simply about you. Having a team creates an opportunity for collective success.

Mentoring

Mentoring relationships can be instrumental. However, their effectiveness is based on a solid foundation where you ultimately own responsibility for your development. Mentoring does not equal relinquishing ownership and decisions. Key questions to consider are:

- Who do you know that would consider your development a priority or worthwhile investment? (Consider multiple resources in different functions, industries or geographical areas.)

- What do you need assistance with? (Define your developmental needs and let your mentor help refine them.)

- How much time outside of normal work hours are you willing to invest in building the mentoring relationship? (Regular work demands might limit availability.)

- Do you need occasional guidance in a single conversation, over a short time period or at regular intervals over a longer time horizon? (Be flexible based on what the mentor is willing and able to give.)

You own your development. Good mentors are excellent complementary resources to help you achieve your goals. They will help guide you on your path based on their experience and expertise.

Sponsorship

Who do you rely on when you need access to key individuals, opportunities, organizations and communities? Of course, it will be someone who already has those relationships. This key individual who plays a powerful role in your development is a sponsor. A sponsor is not to be confused with a mentor. Not every mentor is a sponsor and vice versa. A sponsor is typically a senior executive or widely recognized leader who is highly respected, maintains significant visibility, has strong, extensive connections and leverages considerable influence as your advocate. This person opens the door to your opportunities.

Think, for a moment, about organizations you have worked or volunteered in or communities you are familiar with. Which leaders meet the criteria outlined above? Someone who sponsors you—i.e. connects his or her brand with yours—often markets you to others who are unfamiliar with your character and performance record.

Sponsor relationships might take considerable time and effort to develop. Your strategically invested time, effort and exceptional performance help position you for opportunities to build partnerships with key sponsors. What actions can you take to strengthen your attractiveness to a sponsor?

- **Remain clear about the sponsor's role**. While it is wonderful if you are able to develop friendships resulting from work and community involvement, never forget that this is a professional relationship that will help you move forward. Do not become bound by comfort and decreased assertiveness that clouds your perspective and ability to maintain your sponsor's support.

- **Invest in your leadership presence.** Your language, knowledge, behaviors and appearance are critical elements of your leadership presence. I must underscore their importance because, too often, lack of leadership presence is the nebulous or unspoken "it" that is missing. This remains a common theme in my messaging because it is so critical. Enlist your mentor, coach and Personal Advisory Board for candid feedback. If you need to invest in a leadership coach with expertise in image and presence, it might be one of the best investments you will make with immeasurable returns.

- **Respect your sponsor's time.** I work with executives who are often challenged with preserving a precious resource—time. One highly visible executive remarked, "I give my very best when working with others who can benefit from my experience, knowledge and connections. I really enjoy helping others. But some people will suck the life out of you if you let them. I have started saying 'no' a lot more frequently. If they have no respect for my time, then I must create boundaries." Don't be the "life sucker"!

Remember, given their investment in you—as well as what you will give back to them—it is unlikely that you will have many sponsors. Who are your current or prospective sponsors? What initiatives or projects is your potential sponsor leading that you can become engaged in? What is your sponsor passionate about that you can support?

Coaching

Professional coaching focuses on helping you move forward on your journey. While coaching can be related to your current career or business pursuits, it can easily be focused on new, unexplored endeavors. A professional coach should be supportive, challenging and open to your agenda—not what she wants for you. A coach can offer advice and share experiences, but it is not her role to tell you what *needs* to be done. As I share with my clients, I am here to assist with the excavation process, helping unearth the potential that already exists.

There are many professional coaches in the market. Be sure to talk with several to ensure your styles are complementary. Every coach is not the coach for you; similarly, every client is not the right client for a particular coach. Do not be shy about finding what works for you and moves you forward on your journey.

Having a professional coach as a part of my team was the best investment I made in my personal and professional development. I can only begin to quantify how much time, money and effort was saved with an accountability partner who listened to what I expressed, as well as what I *did not* say, and stretched me to perform at my peak. Had I not partnered with a professional coach when launching The Batie Group, I would have been in the wrong business. I was pursuing what I was *comfortable* with rather than what I truly desired.

🏃 EXCAVATION EXERCISE

How might the following benefit you?

Personal Advisory Board

_____

_____

_____

_____

_____

Mentor

_____

_____

_____

_____

_____

Sponsor

_____

_____

_____

_____

_____

Professional Coach

_____

_____

_____

_____

_____

What attributes would you seek in a:

Personal Advisor

_____

_____

_____

_____

_____

Mentor

_____

_____

_____

_____

_____

Sponsor

_____

_____

_____

_____

_____

Professional Coach

_____

_____

_____

_____

_____

List potential Personal Advisors:

1. _____

2. _____

3. _____

4. _____

5. _____

List potential Mentors:

1. _____

2. _____

3. _____

4. _____

5. _____

List potential Sponsors:

1. _____

2. _____

3. _____

4. _____

5. _____

List potential Professional Coaches:

1. _____

2. _____

3. _____

4. _____

5. _____

CHAPTER 11

VALUE IN THE VISION

"The most pathetic person in the world is someone who has sight, but has no vision."
Helen Keller

You have excellent skills, an impeccable image, a strong foundation and a powerful circle. So, where are you going?

Now that you have given consideration to who you are, what is most important to you, how you see yourself, how others perceive you and who is in your inner circle, what are you moving toward? What is it that you *really* desire?

Sometimes we become so entrenched in what we know, have done or are known for doing that it is difficult for us to see beyond where we are right now. If you are on the right path and simply want to move to a more fulfilling level on your journey, CONGRATULATIONS!! If you are frustrated with or uncertain about where you are right now and are ready to choose a different path, CONGRATULATIONS!! It is important that you recognize where you are even if you are unclear about what you desire and how you are going to get there.

Set aside what you have become comfortable doing for just a moment. I am a realist who is not asking you to toss your job to the side because I know that we all have responsibilities. I simply want you to figuratively set aside what you have done, know how to do with your eyes closed or have become known for doing.

All of your needs are met and nothing is standing in your way. What are you doing with your life?

_____

_____

_____

_____

_____

How are you spending your time?

_____

_____

_____

_____

What impact are you having on others? How are others' lives different because of what you are doing?

Did you notice the tense that those statements and questions were written in? I love the power of present tense. It transports the experience to where you are right now. There is no focus on what you will do or have done but where you *currently* are. That is how I want you to think about your vision. Imagine yourself living it today.

If this exercise makes you a little uncomfortable, that is good. I want your vision to stretch you beyond what is most comfortable. That is how we grow and develop. Discomfort can be a powerful catalyst for the changes you are seeking in your life. *Get comfortable with being uncomfortable.*

CHAPTER 12

ASPIRE TO BE YOU

"The Past: Our cradle, not our prison; there is danger as well as appeal in its glamour. The past is for inspiration, not imitation; for continuation, not repetition."
Israel Zangwill

When I was a young girl, I dreamed of being a teacher and a librarian. They were such important, all-knowing beings. They could silence the room with the sweep of a finger to their tightly perched lips as their eyes peered above their horn-rimmed glasses. Some days, while pretending to be the librarian, complete with a date stamp and cards to check out books, I would pull my hair back with a thick rubber band into a fuzzy, puffy po-nytail. I would then put my mother's old, big glasses on the tip of my nose and drape a cardigan around my shoulders, only se-cured by the top bottom. This was certainly the librarian's look, right? While I had little real insight to teachers' and librarians' full responsibilities, I mimicked who I thought they were and what I assumed it took to be "it"—everything that captured a teacher's or librarian's essence.

Whenever I begin my "librarian dream" story, my husband finishes it for me verbatim. "You would then drape your arms with a cardigan and button it at the top." Have I really told the story *that* often? Am I becoming the very people who used to elicit chuckles from me as they told the story with the same fondness for nostalgia for the "umpteenth" time? As I became the teacher or librarian, I changed the way I spoke, moved across the room, engaged with the "class" (of dolls and stuffed animals), read my books and sat at my desk. Interestingly enough, had I become an elementary school teacher, based on my personality and experiences, it his highly unlikely that I would have been anything like those I mimicked.

Throughout my life, there have been many individuals whose characteristics, behaviors, style, knowledge and wisdom have inspired me. Some I knew well, others I knew only through media and still others were total strangers. Take a moment to think about one person whom you admire.

Who is s/he? _____

What is one characteristic you admire in that person?

_____

_____

How might you leverage that influence to be better or more effective?

_____

_____

_____

_____

Here is my personal example:

MY INFLUENCER—DR. MAYA ANGELOU

Characteristic—Clear, concise and creative speaker

How I leverage her influence—I am mindful about how I speak. Especially when I am nervous or in a tense situation, I intentionally slow my speaking, think about the impact I want my words to have, enunciate clearly and focus on value versus volume. Additionally, I use personal experiences to make whatever I am sharing more relatable.

I will *never* speak or write like Dr. Maya. *Never*. She already has that mastered. What I *will* do is use what I have learned through watching and listening to her as well as reading her writings to more fully and effectively be the very best ME!

As a leader who helps other leaders experience their full potential, I am often asked how one can "be" like someone else. "How can I have her confidence?" While it is good to use someone as a model, the greatest disservice you can do to yourself is trying to *be* like that person. Your personality, thoughts, behaviors, experiences and knowledge make you the beautifully unique person you are. Is that *really* worth sacrificing the greatest resource you have in order to be like someone else? How much of their journey are you willing to mimic to get their outcome? We are shaped by our experiences which cannot be duplicated.

I know it is tempting, especially when you see someone who is polished, poised, professional and successful. When they are able to accomplish goals that you have dreamed of or have overcome challenges that you struggle with, it might be even more tempting. "I want to be just like that." I always enjoy hearing Oprah Winfrey talk about the period in her life where she mimicked Barbara Walters—the way she talked, sat and interviewed guests. She was so inspired by what Barbara Walters represented to her that she wanted to *be* like her.

Attempting to BE like someone else is a short-term solution to achieving long-term success. What we learn from others certainly can help us be more effective at being who we *are*.

What are the differences between mimicking and inspiring? Merriam Webster defines them as follows:

- Mimic—to imitate closely or impersonate;
- Inspire—to influence, move or guide.

How do you distinguish imitating versus being inspired by others?

Think about product advertisements. Have you seen the commercials that tout how much product A is like product B? Product B is the benchmark for style, fuel efficiency, features, performance, etc. Why would I not simply purchase Product B?

It reminds me of the fragrance product line whose tag line was, "If you like (designer fragrance), you'll love (designer imitation fragrance)." I remember having a favorite among the imitations "way back when". I purchased it because I could not afford the designer fragrance but wanted to smell like I could. I was convinced that it was impossible to tell the difference.

Well, little did I know but my body chemistry did not mix with that "if you like/you'll love" fragrance. While out with a group, one friend began sniffing and looking around. With a confused look that I will never forget she asked, "Does anyone else smell insect spray?" Needless to say, my love affair with the "if you like/you'll love" products ended that night! Until I could afford the real thing years later, I settled for perfumes that fit into my budget AND smelled good, while occasionally visiting the local department store to experience the authentic product for the day.

> *"Do not go where the path may lead,*
> *go instead where there is no path and leave a trail."*
> **Ralph Waldo Emerson**

There is great value in learning from and being inspired by others. I encourage you to fully leverage what they do well by modeling their impact—not their person—as is often witnessed through their passion, enthusiasm, commitment to excellence and living their core values.

EXCAVATION EXERCISE:

Who inspires you? What is it about them that you admire?

_____

_____

_____

_____

_____

_____

_____

_____

_____

_____

_____

_____

_____

_____

_____

_____

What characteristics and qualities do you possess that others often compliment? For example, do you have a knack for quickly connecting with others? Bringing a story to life? Sense of humor?

1. _____

2. _____

3. _____

4. _____

5. _____

What skills, knowledge and experiences do you have that others value and seek from you?

1. _____

2. _____

3. _____

4. _____

5. _____

How might you use what you already possess plus others' inspiration to more effectively and fully be YOU?

CHAPTER 13

· · · · · · · · · · · · · · · · · · · ·

THE PROOF IS IN THE PUDDING

"Excellence is an art won by training and habituation...
We are what we repeatedly do.
Excellence, then, is not an act but a habit."
Aristotle

Have you ever experienced excellent service? You know... the kind of service that you can hardly wait to share with others? In some cases, years after that experience, we recount the story to others. These situations are generally seen as "above and beyond" rare instances.

In working with business leaders, particularly around branding, marketing and business development, our early discussions often lead to one question: "How do we increase our profitability?" In other words, what can you do that few others are doing to set yourself apart from the competition, resulting in increased opportunities?

Powerful Impact

Recently, I went to a fast food restaurant, placing my drive-thru order five minutes before closing. Cheerfully, the young lady welcomed me, took my order, confirmed my request and told me that she looked forward to seeing me at the window. As the young lady continued taking other orders, the store manager gave me my freshly prepared food (it was actually HOT!). "Any time I have ever been here, this staff is consistently courteous, professional and such a pleasure to deal with," I shared with the manager. She graciously thanked me, told me how much the staff would appreciate hearing that and reiterated how much that meant to her before I pulled away.

Why has this business experienced tremendous success, even in a so-called down economy? Because their performance aligns with their corporate purpose to positively impact everyone who experiences their brand. Unlike another restaurant with similar potential but varying results, they simply deliver what they promise—consistently! That IS your brand.

One of my favorite business books is *The Personal Touch: What You Really Need to Succeed in Today's Fast-paced Business World* by Terrie Williams. The book has been around for a while but the principles are timeless. In her chapter on reputation, Terrie reminds us that "to establish or enhance a good reputation, you must combine... character-building ingredients including hard work, persistence, honesty and disdain for mediocrity..." If you really want to set yourself and your business apart, begin with delivering what you promise, when you said it would be done, with excellence and an appreciation for those who help make you and your business successful. Everything else should be added to that foundation. I know it sounds basic but many organizations and leaders do not deliver according to that standard.

Before discussing new and different strategies, I go back to the foundation—the basics—with my clients:

- What have you promised to deliver to your customers and employees? When you are courting and recruiting them, what promises do you make?

- How consistent are you at fulfilling those promises?

- What are your organization's best practices, the personal touches that you add to increase the value to your customer?

- What are the specific gaps in what you have promised and what you are delivering?

- How do you plan to align your performance with their expectations?

Sadly, good, solid service graciously delivered with the customer's best interests in mind is so infrequent that it seems more like an "above and beyond" effort when you get it. Excellence is reflected in your execution, not flashy marketing copy, the latest trend or short-term fixes. Your actions, results and profitability are positively correlated. What you do, and how you do it, speaks louder than any slick marketing materials or catchy slogans. The proof is in the performance!

EXCAVATION EXERCISE

As a personal brand, what are the top three areas requiring your attention in order to more effectively: 1) access the opportunities you desire; 2) consistently serve those who value what you deliver; and 3) achieve your priority goals?

1. _____

_____

_____

2. _____

_____

_____

3. _____

_____

_____

What skills, knowledge and experiences are you willing to obtain and/or enhance to ensure you can effectively be the brand—deliver the experience you promise—that you desire to be?

1. _____

_____

_____

2. _____

_____

_____

3. _____

_____

_____

4. _____

_____

_____

5. _____

_____

_____

CHAPTER 14

· · · · · · · · · · · · · · · · · · ·

BE THE BRAND

"Don't wait. The time will never be just right."
Napoleon Hill

Having an idea, creating a plan to execute it, building support systems and understanding how who you are contributes to the plan's success are all noble. The biggest hurdle we are often confronted with is the decision to move forward.

How many times have you attended conferences, participated in training sessions, read books, downloaded audio programs and purchased products yet you are still struggling with experiencing a life that fulfills you? Some call it "preparation paralysis"—preparing but never really moving forward.

I do not want this to be another book you read, put on the shelf and go back to where you were. After serving as a Business Strategist and Executive Coach for talented leaders around the globe, I know the realities that face you when you close this book. Some of the stories I have heard are:

> **"I wish I had time to make these changes in my life."**

> **"Once the kids are self-sufficient, the house is clean, I lose these last 20 pounds and I get some of these other responsibilities off of my plate, I will be ready."**

> **"Money is tight. The economy is down. Employment is uncertain. When the economic outlook brightens, I will become more focused."**

> **"I have heard this before. I know I need to do something but I just don't have the energy."**

> **"I have so far to go that I do not know where to begin."**

> **"The last time I started down this path, I failed."**

> **"Suppose it becomes difficult and overwhelming?"**

If you had nothing to lose, what would you do differently? Really... what steps would you take—one at a time—to finally move to a greater satisfaction level in your life.

At its core, your brand is directly correlated to who you are, how *you think* about who you are and how much attention you are willing to give to yourself to be better. Yes, others will perceive you based on what they know, see, are told and experience. However, the primary person responsible for maximizing your brand is YOU!

Based on who you desire to be, what <u>ONE</u> action are you willing to take to move from idea to action?

_____

_____

_____

_____

_____

When will you take action?

_____

_____

_____

Who are you willing to ask to support you?

_____

_____

_____

When will you ask for that support?

_____

_____

_____

What is your primary concern about moving forward?

_____

_____

_____

_____

_____

What decisions will you make to move past this concern?

_____

_____

_____

_____

_____

CONGRATULATIONS to you for having the courage to take this next step! I am excited about where this journey will take you.

My deepest desire is to know that you will confront your mental hurdles, move past them, dig deep within yourself, touch just one gem that has been planted inside of you, hold it up to the light and watch the light shine brilliantly through you to the rest of the world.

"Success is not defined by your wings but by your courage to leap from the cliff's edge and fly!"
LaFern K. Batie, MBA

Keep soaring, Eagle!

Please be sure to visit us at:
www.TheBatieGroup.com

Be the first to know about LaFern Batie's speaking appearances as well as our latest workshops and products by signing up to receive The Eagle's Perch, a complimentary leadership resource filled with practical resources with a powerful impact.

Do you desire additional professional development resources or want to request to have LaFern K. Batie speak for your organization?

E-mail us at info@TheBatieGroup.com;

or

Submit an online request form via

www.TheBatieGroup.com/professional-speaking-php;

or

Call our offices via (888) 735-1716.

BONUS RESOURCES

The *Marketing Brand YOU®: Moving from Chaos to Clarity Resource Guide* is a BONUS personal development tool available to all readers. The following instructions will assist you in easily accessing your <u>complimentary</u> guide:

- Go to www.TheBatieGroup.com/products.php;
- Click on the Marketing Brand YOU®: Moving from Chaos to Clarity Resource Guide;
- Enter your name and e-mail address;
- Access to the guide will be immediately provided.

To participate in our high-impact and practical **workshops** to help you move forward with other highly motivated leaders, explore our offerings via:

www.TheBatieGroup.com/workshops.php